Guide Dogs for the Blind

by Alice Boynton

LOOK!
BOOKS™

Red Chair Press   Egremont, Massachusetts

Look! Books are produced and published by Red Chair Press:

Red Chair Press LLC   PO Box 333   South Egremont, MA 01258-0333

www.redchairpress.com

Red Chair Press dedicates this book
to Brandi, Nicole, Halla, Abbey, and Fergie and the
thousands of helpers provided by The Seeing Eye ®.

Publisher's Cataloging-In-Publication Data

Names: Boynton, Alice Benjamin

Title: Guide dogs for the blind / by Alice Boynton.

Description: Egremont, Massachusetts : Red Chair Press, [2018] | Series: Look! books : Animals that help us | Interest age level: 004-007. | Includes Now You Know fact-boxes, a glossary, and resources for additional reading. | Includes index. | Summary: "You know that pets can be fun. But some dogs, horses, pigs, and more have important jobs to do. With Animals That Help Us young readers will discover how animals help us stay safe. Readers will discover how dogs, and even some horses, are trained to help the blind stay safe and secure in their daily lives."-- Provided by publisher.

Identifiers: ISBN 978-1-63440-315-3 (library hardcover) | ISBN 978-1-63440-363-4 (paperback) | ISBN 978-1-63440-321-4 (ebook)

Subjects: LCSH: Guide dogs--Juvenile literature. | CYAC: Guide dogs.

Classification: LCC HV1780 .B69 2018 | DDC 362.4183 [E]--dc23

LCCN 2017947557

Photo credits: Cover, p. 1, 5, 19, 22, 23, 24: Shutterstock; p. 3 © Sergio Azenha/ Alamy; p. 7: © William Mullins/Alamy; p. 9: © Pluto/Alamy; p. 11: Getty Images; p. 11: © JUNG YEON-JE/Getty Images; p. 13, 17: © Marmaduke St. John/Alamy; p. 15: © REUTERS/Alamy; p. 21: © TERRY BLACKMAN/Alamy

Printed in the United States of America

0718 1P CGF18

Table of Contents

What's the Job?

Guide dogs make it easier for **blind** people to get around. That's their job. How do these guide dogs learn to do it?

Good to Know

The blind are people who cannot see. There are more than 60,000 students in the United States who are blind.

4

Labradors are smart and calm. They like to work, too.

Puppy Kindergarten

A guide dog starts **training** when it is a puppy. It gets used to different people and places. It learns to be well-behaved. *No chewing the rug, please!*

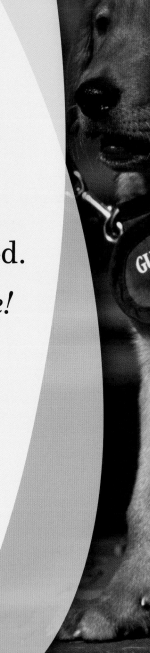

The jacket tells people,
I'm in training.

Guide Dog in Training

Then the puppy goes to training classes. It gets used to wearing a harness. It practices guiding a person around any dangers on the street. At first, the puppy may train with people who can see.

harness

The puppy also practices going up and down stairs. There may be crowds. But the dog must stay **calm**. Other times, it learns to just lie quietly. The dog must be quiet when the blind person is at work or at school.

Blind people know where they want to go. They tell the dog by giving **commands**. The dog learns what each command means. Then it can lead the way. *Smart dog!*

List of Commands

Sit............... Sit down
Down .... Lay down
Stay............. Don't move
Come .... Come to me
Forward ..... Start walking
Right .... Turn right
Left .... Turn left
Hup-up........ Hurry
Steady .... Slow down

13

Graduation!

After months of training, the dog is ready to work. It meets the blind person it will live with. Before long, they will be best buddies. After all, the blind owner and the dog will be together night and day.

15

On the Job

Guide dogs are allowed to go everywhere. You may see them on planes and in stores. This guide dog and owner are in a restaurant.

When crossing a street, the dog halts, or stops, at the curb. The blind person hears the traffic stop. "Forward," he says.

If there's no danger, the dog starts to walk.

But this time there's a car speeding around the corner. Danger! The dog refuses to go. The owner trusts her dog. So she stops too. Whew! *Good work partner!*

It's safe to cross.

21

If you see a guide dog, remember that it's working. Don't try to pet it. Later at home, the owner will take off the dog's harness. Then the dog knows it is okay to relax. *Time to play!*

Good to Know

Guide dogs know that once the harness goes on, it is time to work. You should never try to pet or play with a dog in its harness. Ask the owner first.

Words to Keep

blind: not able to see

calm: not upset

command: an order to do something

training: teaching to do something

Learn More at the Library

Books (Check out these books to learn more.)

Buddy, The First Seeing Eye Dog (Hello Reader) by Eva Moore. Scholastic, 1996.

Seeing-Eye Dogs (We Work! Animals with Jobs) by Jennifer Fretland VanVoorst. Bearport Publishing Company, 2014.

Web Sites (Ask an adult to show you these web sites.)

Guide Dog Puppies video
http://channel.nationalgeographic.com/wild/videos/guide-dog-puppies/

The Seeing Eye Children's video
https://www.youtube.com/watch?v=z4n0N4tj0MI

Index

About the Author

Alice Boynton has 20 years
of experience in the classroom.
She knows many guide dogs in
her New York City neighborhood.